Times to Remember

Introduction

There are many ways for us to remember wonderful events, but few are as special as these personal cross-stitch designs memorializing the occasions that highlight our lives.

In *Times to Remember*, we wander through your life, from the announcement of birth, through first birthdays, teen birthdays and adult birthdays. We dedicate a section to family vacations and the arrival of favorite pets.

Next we recall high school and college graduations, bridal showers, weddings and anniversaries. Finally we reflect on family with reunion designs and an ornate Family Tree.

In each section, we provide designs for announcements as well as gift ideas and novelty souvenirs for the occasion. You will enjoy stitching these designs both to remember your own events, and as gifts for your friends' special days.

Contents

You will enjoy announcing your newborn with personalized designs for baby girl and baby boy. You'll also find several special novelties for baby, including bibs, sip cup, burp towel, wash mitt, bottle cover and wraps for organizing baby's room.

In this chapter, we recognize first birthdays for little boy and little girl.

Teen birthdays are remembered with bright and colorful celebration novelties, including journal and diary covers, bookmarks, switchplate and makeup case.

We honor adults as well, with announcements and small gift and party ideas.

Some of our favorite times to remember include family vacations. In this chapter, we highlight some popular vacations with designs for photo album and scrapbook covers, along with mini souvenirs, such as bag tags, coasters, magnets and bag clips.

Honor your new cat or dog with his own welcome announcement. We've also included a variety of ideas for canister wraps, small framed designs and cards featuring some favorite felines or canines.

Times to Remember

Editor: Bobbie Matela
Managing Editor: Marion Noble
Associate Editor: Cathy Reef
Technical Editor: Christina Wilson
Copy Supervisor: Michelle Beck
Copy Editors: Conor Allen, Nicki Lehman

Photography: Tammy Christian, Carl Clark, Christena Green, Matt Owen
Photography Stylist: Tammy Nussbaum

Publishing Services Manager: Brenda Gallmeyer
Cover Design: Karen Allen
Graphic Artist: Pam Gregory
Production Assistant: Marj Morgan
Technical Artist: Chad Summers

Chief Executive Officer: John Robinson
Publishing Director: David Mckee
Book Marketing Director: Craig Scott
Editorial Director: Vivian Rothe
Publishing Services Director: Brenda R. Wendling

Printed in the United States of America
First Printing: 2005
Library of Congress Number: 2004110520
ISBN: 1-59012-103-1

Designers: Linda Gillum and Donna Yuen

Thank you to the following companies who supplied products for our models:
Beacon Chemical Company, Bernina® of America, Charles Craft, Crafter's Pride, DMC Corporation, Fairfield Processing Corp., Jeanette Crews Designs, Inc., Kreinik, MCG Textitles, Northcott Silk, Sudberry House and Zweigart.

Photographed models were stitched by: Debra Brown, Barbara Chancy, Betty Curran, Maryann Donovan, Faye Gibson, Lorraine Giera, Ellen Harnden, Traci Lis, Helen McClaine, Maxine Meadows, Pam Mollahan, Barbara Moore, Kim Nelson, Rita Noggle, Loretta Norman, Mary Alice Patsko, Robyn Purta, Lee Ann Tibbals and Heather Walker

TOLL FREE ORDER LINE or to request a free catalog (800) 582-6643
Customer Service (800) 282-6643, Fax (800) 882-6643 • Visit www.AnniesAttic.com

2   3   4   5   6   7   8   9

Welcome Baby Girl

Design Size: 108 wide x 133 high

CROSS-STITCH

DMC		Anchor	
164	U	261	Light forest green
335	#	38	Rose
350	♥	11	Medium coral
553	−	98	Violet
554	$	96	Light violet
743	☆	302	Medium yellow
745	1	300	Light pale yellow
807	⌘	168	Peacock blue
818	/	23	Baby pink
948	✓	1011	Very light peach
988	♣	243	Medium forest green
3326	S	36	Light rose
3761	O	928	Light sky blue
3799	⋈	236	Very dark pewter gray
3853	◐	1003	Dark autumn gold
3854	<	313	Medium autumn gold
blanc	·	2	White

FRENCH KNOTS

DMC		Anchor	
335	●	38	Rose
975	●	355	Dark golden brown
3799	●	236	Very dark pewter gray

BACKSTITCH

DMC		Anchor	
335	—	38	Rose (2 strands)
350	—	11	Medium coral
975	—	355	Dark golden brown
988	—	243	Medium forest green
3799	—	236	Very dark pewter gray

LAZY DAISY

DMC		Anchor	
988	—	243	Medium forest green (2 strands)

Model was stitched on 14-count antique white Aida fabric and is shown in a lilac 10 x 12-inch frame. For lettering, use rose (2 strands).

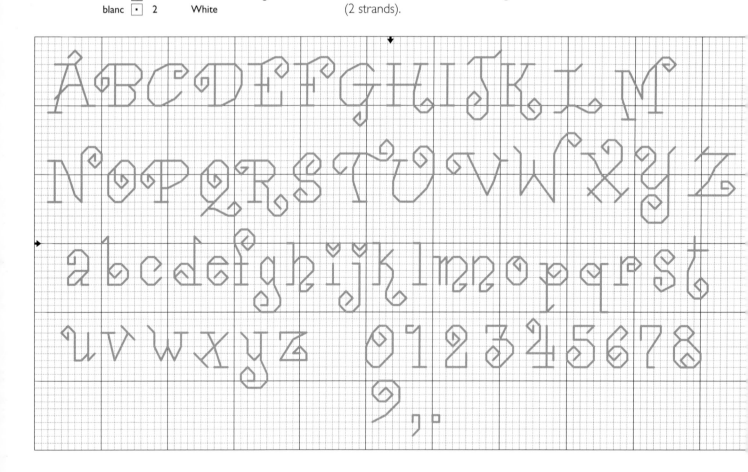

Welcome Baby Boy

Design Size: 108 wide x 135 high

CROSS-STITCH

DMC		Anchor	
164	?	261	Light forest green
208	#	110	Very dark lavender
209	)	109	Dark lavender
347	♥	1025	Very dark salmon
350	⅔	11	Medium coral
352	1	9	Light coral
415	–	398	Pearl gray
535	■	401	Very light ash gray
725	0	305	Topaz
727	~	293	Very light topaz
742	☆	303	Light tangerine
762	$	234	Very light pearl gray
826	✳	161	Medium blue
827	◇	160	Very light blue
945	◆◆	881	Tawny
951	··	1010	Light tawny
975	⊗	355	Dark golden brown
976	➡	1001	Medium golden brown

CROSS-STITCH

DMC		Anchor	
988	♣	243	Medium forest green
3827	⬇	311	Pale golden brown
blanc	·	2	White

FRENCH KNOT

DMC		Anchor	
350	●	11	Medium coral
535	●	401	Very light ash gray
727	●	293	Very light topaz

BACKSTITCH

DMC		Anchor	
350	–	11	Medium coral (2 strands)
535	–	401	Very light ash gray
826	–	161	Medium blue (2 strands)
975	–	355	Dark golden brown
986	–	246	Very dark forest green

STRAIGHT STITCH

DMC		Anchor	
350	–	11	Medium coral

Model was stitched on 14-count antique white Aida fabric and is shown in a light blue 10 x 12-inch frame.

For lettering, refer to alphabet and use medium blue.

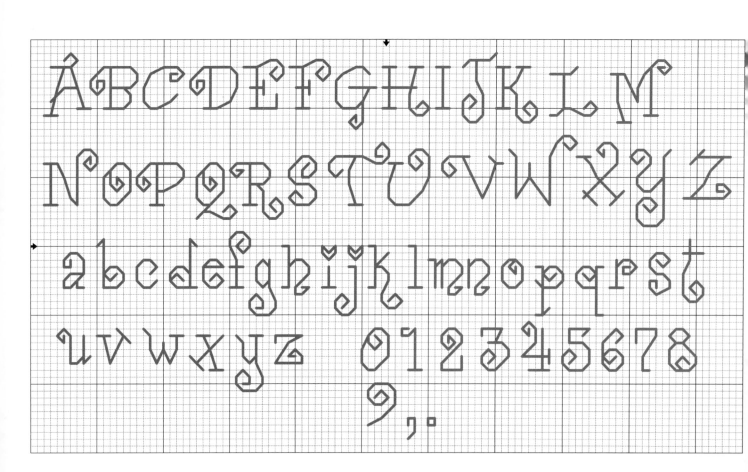

_____ lbs _____ ozs

Lion and Friends

Design Size: 52 wide x 51 high

CROSS-STITCH

DMC		Anchor	
209	1	109	Dark lavender
351	6	10	Coral
352	5	9	Light coral
402	8	1047	Very light mahogany
776	⬇	24	Medium pink
799	◆◆	136	Medium delft blue
800	$	144	Pale delft blue
945	◇	881	Tawny
951	⸙	1010	Light tawny
3371	■	382	Black brown

FRENCH KNOT

DMC		Anchor	
300	●	352	Very dark mahogany
351	●	10	Coral
799	●	136	Medium delft blue
3371	●	382	Black brown

BACKSTITCH

DMC		Anchor	
300	—	352	Very dark mahogany (2 strands)
351	—	10	Coral
3371	—	382	Black brown (2 strands)

STRAIGHT STITCH

DMC		Anchor	
3371	—	382	Black brown (2 strands)

Model was stitched on a 14-count quilted white bib with pink gingham trim.

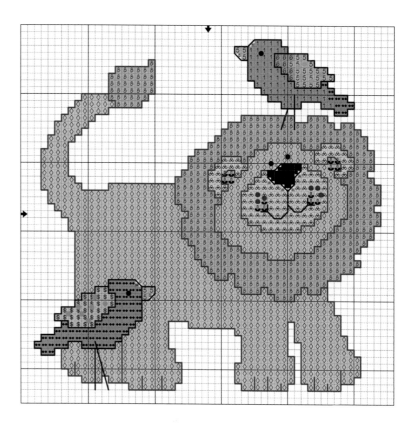

Elephant

Design Size: 35 wide x 25 high

CROSS-STITCH

DMC		Anchor	
310	■	403	Black
318	+	399	Light steel gray
414	$	235	Dark steel gray
415	/	398	Pearl gray
blanc	·	2	White

BACKSTITCH

DMC		Anchor	
310	—	403	Black (2 strands)
3799	—	236	Very dark pewter gray

Model was stitched on a 14-count terry drool bib with yellow gingham trim.

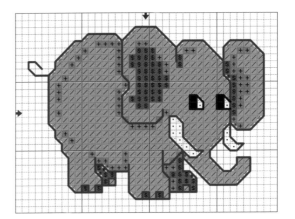

Alligator

Design Size: 61 wide x 11 high

CROSS-STITCH

DMC		Anchor	
310	■	403	Black
318	+	399	Light steel gray
986	■	246	Very dark forest green
989	✳	242	Forest green
blanc	·	2	White

BACKSTITCH

DMC		Anchor	
310	—	403	Black (2 strands)
433	—	358	Medium brown

Model was stitched on a 14-count terry burp towel with yellow gingham trim.

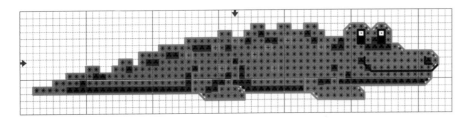

CROSS-STITCH

DMC		Anchor	
519	⌘	1038	Sky blue
666	◆◆	46	Bright Christmas red
704	⟮	256	Bright chartreuse

BACKSTITCH

3799	━	236	Very dark pewter gray

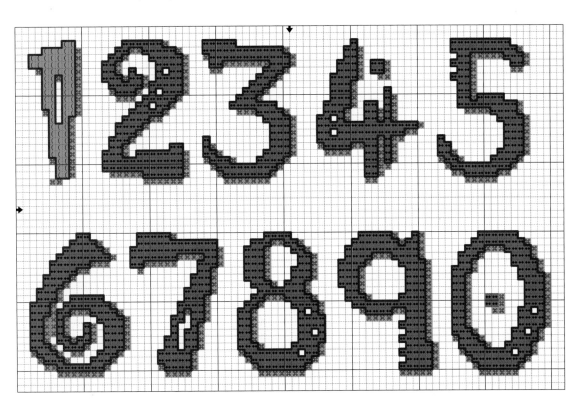

My Diary

Design Size: 79 wide x 51 high

CROSS-STITCH

DMC		Anchor	
209	✳	109	Dark lavender
519	⌘	1038	Sky blue
601	◪	57	Dark cranberry
604	4	55	Light cranberry
666	#	46	Bright Christmas red
741	$	304	Medium tangerine
743	☆	302	Medium yellow
745	╱	300	Light pale yellow
792	●	941	Dark cornflower blue
913	2	204	Medium Nile green
996	✛	433	Medium electric blue
3348	–	264	Light yellow green
3839	╱	176	Medium lavender blue

BACKSTITCH

601	—	57	Dark cranberry (2 strands)
792	—	941	Dark cornflower blue (2 strands)
3799	—	236	Very dark pewter gray
3814	—	1074	Aquamarine (2 strands)

STRAIGHT STITCH

743	—	302	Medium yellow (2 strands)

Model is stitched on 14-count natural Aida fabric and is shown on a 5 x 7-inch journal with red trim.

Happy Birthday

Design Size: 94 wide x 66 high

CROSS-STITCH

DMC		Anchor	
162	◆◆	9159	Ultra very light blue
164	=	261	Light forest green
208	⊞	110	Very dark lavender
209	⠿	109	Dark lavender
211	∧	342	Light lavender
310	■	403	Black
550	■	102	Very dark violet
743	☆	302	Medium yellow
745	⦙⦙⦙	300	Light pale yellow
824	■	164	Very dark blue
826	⬇	161	Medium blue

CROSS-STITCH

DMC		Anchor	
890	■	218	Ultra dark pistachio green
939	■	152	Very dark navy blue
988	◀	243	Medium forest green
3685	✖	1028	Dark mauve
3687	7	68	Mauve
3688	8	66	Medium mauve
3689	9	49	Light mauve
3755	⊗	140	Baby blue
3820	⬮	306	Dark straw
blanc	⬡	1	White

FRENCH KNOT

DMC		Anchor	
3799	●	236	Very dark pewter gray

BACKSTITCH

DMC		Anchor	
550	—	102	Very dark violet
824	—	164	Very dark blue
988	—	243	Medium forest green
3685	—	1028	Dark mauve
3799	—	236	Very dark pewter gray

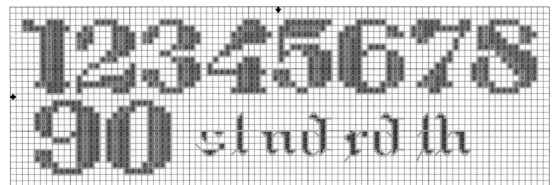

Model was stitched on 14-count antique white Aida fabric and is shown in an 8 x 10-inch dark blue frame.

For numerals, refer to chart and color key.

Teapot Candle Wrap

Design Size: 67 wide x 40 high

CROSS-STITCH

DMC		Anchor	
208	▦	110	Very dark lavender
209	7	109	Dark lavender
211	∧	342	Light lavender
743	☆	302	Medium yellow
745	◇	300	Light pale yellow
890	■	218	Ultra dark pistachio green
988	♥	243	Medium forest green
3687	◆◆	68	Mauve
3688	⦀	66	Medium mauve
3755	∞	140	Baby blue
3820	▼	306	Dark straw
blanc	9	2	White

BACKSTITCH

DMC		Anchor	
824	—	164	Very dark blue
3799	—	236	Very dark pewter gray

Model was stitched on 14-count white Aida fabric, wrapped around a canister and trimmed with light blue rickrack.

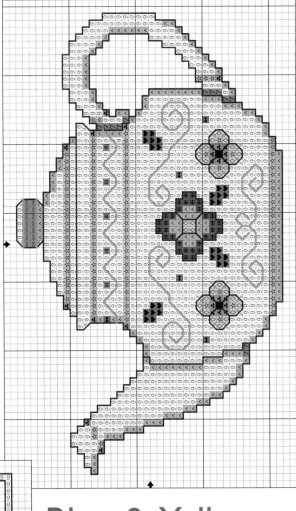

Pansy Teacup Napkin

Design Size: 25 wide x 24 high

CROSS-STITCH

DMC		Anchor	
164	✕	261	Light forest green
209	7	109	Dark lavender
211	∧	342	Light lavender
310	■	403	Black
743	☆	302	Medium yellow
745	◇	300	Light pale yellow
826	⬇	161	Medium blue
890	■	218	Ultra dark pistachio green
988	♥	243	Medium forest green
3685	✕	1028	Dark mauve
3687	◆◆	68	Mauve
3688	⦀	66	Medium mauve
3689	✣	49	Light mauve
3755	∞	140	Baby blue
3820	▼	306	Dark straw
blanc	9	2	White

BACKSTITCH

DMC		Anchor	
988	—	243	Medium forest green
3799	—	236	Very dark pewter gray

Model was stitched on a pre-finished 14-count white Aida napkin.

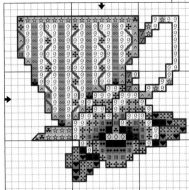

Blue & Yellow Teacup Napkin

Design Size: 28 wide x 18 high

CROSS-STITCH

DMC		Anchor	
209	7	109	Dark lavender
211	∧	342	Light lavender
743	☆	302	Medium yellow
826	⬇	161	Medium blue
3755	∞	140	Baby blue
3820	▼	306	Dark straw
blanc	9	2	White

BACKSTITCH

DMC		Anchor	
743	—	302	Medium yellow (2 strands)
3799	—	236	Very dark pewter gray

Checkerboard Teacup Napkin

Design Size: 26 wide x 16 high

CROSS-STITCH

DMC		Anchor	
209	7	109	Dark lavender
211	∧	342	Light lavender
743	☆	302	Medium yellow
3685	■	1028	Dark mauve
3687	◆◆	68	Mauve
3820	▼	306	Dark straw
blanc	9	2	White

BACKSTITCH

DMC		Anchor	
3799	—	236	Very dark pewter gray

Model was stitched on a pre-finished 14-count white Aida napkin.

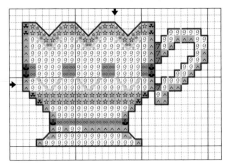

Model was stitched on a pre-finished 14-count white Aida napkin.

Butterfly Coaster

Design Size: 39 wide x 38 high

CROSS-STITCH

DMC		Anchor	
164	ß	261	Light forest green
208	▦	110	Very dark lavender
209	∞	109	Dark lavender
211	∧	342	Light lavender
743	☆	302	Medium yellow
745	◆◆	300	Light pale yellow
824	●	164	Very dark blue
988	7	243	Medium forest green
3688	$	66	Medium mauve
3689	%	49	Light mauve
3755	⊞	140	Baby blue

BACKSTITCH

3799	—	236	Very dark pewter gray

Model was stitched on 14-count white Aida fabric and is shown in a 3-inch pre-finished acrylic coaster.

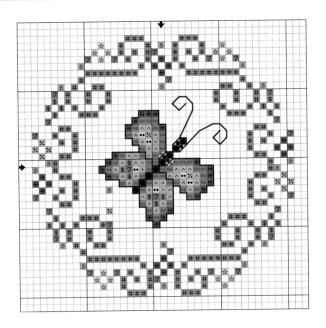

Pansy Notepad

Design Size: 52 wide x 73 high

CROSS-STITCH

DMC		Anchor	
162	−	9159	Ultra very light blue
164	8	261	Light forest green
208	⊞	110	Very dark lavender
209	∞	109	Dark lavender
211	∧	342	Light lavender
310	■	403	Black
550	■	102	Very dark violet
743	☆	302	Medium yellow
745	◆◆	300	Light pale yellow
826	⬇	161	Medium blue
890	■	218	Ultra dark pistachio green
988	7	243	Medium forest green
3685	▨	1028	Dark mauve
3687	▨	68	Mauve
3688	$	66	Medium mauve
3689	%.	49	Light mauve
3755	⧉	140	Baby blue
3799	▨	236	Very dark pewter gray
3820	❚	306	Dark straw

FRENCH KNOT

824	●	164	Very dark blue

BACKSTITCH

824	−	164	Very dark blue (2 strands)
890	−	218	Ultra dark pistachio green (2 strands)
3799	−	236	Very dark pewter gray

Model was stitched on a 4 x 6¼-inch
14-count vinyl weave insert, shown in a
pre-finished 5¾ x 7¾-inch notepad.

Fisherman's Address Book

Design Size: 51 wide x 78 high

CROSS-STITCH

DMC		Anchor	
211	)	342	Light lavender
356	◆◆	5975	Medium terra-cotta
433	◫	358	Medium brown
469	▦	267	Avocado green
498	▼	1005	Dark Christmas red
535	◩	401	Very light ash gray
743	8	302	Medium yellow
745	^	300	Light pale yellow
758	−	868	Very light terra-cotta
818	I	23	Baby pink
834	✳	874	Very light golden olive
938	■	381	Ultra dark coffee brown
3326	5	36	Light rose
3362	▮	263	Dark pine green
3364	⋈	260	Pine green
3747	:	120	Very light blue violet
3811	∅	1060	Very light turquoise
3848	◧	187	Medium teal green
3849	⌘	186	Light teal green
blanc	·	2	White

BACKSTITCH

DMC		Anchor	
356	−	5975	Medium terra-cotta
535	−	401	Very light ash gray
742	−	303	Light tangerine
745	−	300	Light pale yellow
938	−	381	Ultra dark coffee brown

STRAIGHT STITCH

DMC		Anchor	
433	−	358	Medium brown
469	−	267	Avocado green
743	−	302	Medium yellow
938	−	381	Ultra dark coffee brown

Model was stitched on a 4 x 6¼-inch vinyl weave insert, shown in a pre-finished 5¾ x 7¾-inch address book.

Life Preserver Coaster

Design Size: 29 wide x 28 high

CROSS-STITCH

DMC		Anchor	
435	▲	1046	Very light brown
498	▼	1005	Dark Christmas red
3747	:	120	Very light blue violet
blanc	·	2	White

BACKSTITCH

DMC		Anchor	
938	−	381	Ultra dark coffee brown

Model was stitched on 14-count natural Aida fabric and is shown in a 3½-inch acrylic coaster.

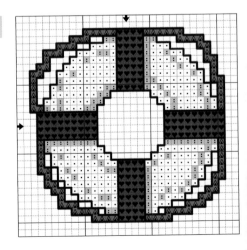

Marlin Switchplate

Design Size: 54 wide x 77 high

CROSS-STITCH

DMC		Anchor	
209	✿	109	Dark lavender
210	⫴	108	Medium lavender
211	)	342	Light lavender
498	♥	1005	Dark Christmas red
745	∧	300	Light pale yellow
775	⁒	128	Very light baby blue
813	3	161	Light blue
824	■	164	Very dark blue
826	✕	161	Medium blue
827	U	160	Very light blue
834	✳	874	Very light golden olive
938	■	381	Ultra dark coffee brown
3747	⫶	120	Very light blue violet
3811	∅	1060	Very light turquoise
3848	⌛	187	Medium teal green
3849	⌘	186	Light teal green
blanc	·	2	White

BACKSTITCH

DMC		Anchor	
742	—	303	Light tangerine
824	—	164	Very dark blue
938	—	381	Ultra dark coffee brown

STRAIGHT STITCH

DMC		Anchor	
938	—	381	Ultra dark coffee brown

Model was stitched on 14-count white Aida fabric and is shown in an acrylic switchplate.

Anchor's Aweigh

Design Size: 20 wide x 26 high

CROSS-STITCH

DMC		Anchor	
433	▦	358	Medium brown
435	◣	1046	Very light brown
743	8	302	Medium yellow

BACKSTITCH

DMC		Anchor	
938	—	381	Ultra dark coffee brown

Model was stitched on 14-count natural Aida fabric and is shown in a 3½-inch acrylic coaster.

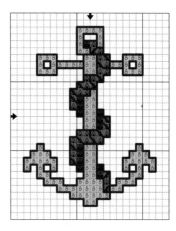

Vacation Memories

Chapter 3

Statue of Liberty

Design Size: 13 wide x 29 high

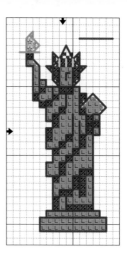

CROSS-STITCH

DMC		Anchor	
743	☆	302	Medium yellow
993	L	1070	Light aquamarine
3814	%	1074	Aquamarine

BACKSTITCH

DMC		Anchor	
312	—	979	Very dark baby blue (2 strands)
433	—	358	Medium brown
720	—	326	Dark orange spice (2 strands)
743	—	302	Medium yellow

Model was stitched on 14-count Aida fabric, shown in a 2¼ x 3½-inch acrylic keychain.

For year of vacation, use numerals on page 47 with medium brown.

Liberty Bell

Design Size: 15 wide x 20 high

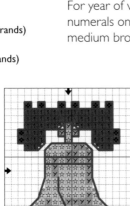

CROSS-STITCH

DMC		Anchor	
433	1	358	Medium brown
535	◈	401	Very light ash gray
741	Y	304	Medium tangerine
743	☆	302	Medium yellow

BACKSTITCH

DMC		Anchor	
433	—	358	Medium brown

Model was stitched on 14-count natural Aida fabric, shown in a 2⅝-inch acrylic magnet.

For year of vacation, use numerals on page 47 with medium brown.

Pink Flamingo

Design Size: 19 wide x 25 high

CROSS-STITCH

DMC		Anchor	
335	▦	38	Rose
535	◈	401	Very light ash gray
745	~	300	Light pale yellow
3326	V	36	Light rose

FRENCH KNOT

DMC		Anchor	
433	●	358	Medium brown

BACKSTITCH

DMC		Anchor	
433	—	358	Medium brown

Model was stitched on 14-count natural fabric and is shown in a 3½-inch acrylic magnet.

For year and place of vacation, use numerals on page 47, upper case alphabet on page 114 and lower case alphabet on page 88 with medium brown.

Southwest

Design Size: 31 wide x 28 high

CROSS-STITCH

DMC		Anchor	
535	◈	401	Very light ash gray
647	5	1040	Medium beaver gray
743	☆	302	Medium yellow
987	4	244	Dark forest green

BACKSTITCH

DMC		Anchor	
433	—	358	Medium brown

Model was stitched on 14-count Aida fabric, shown in an acrylic flashlight keychain.

Casino

Design Size: 46 wide x 23 high

CROSS-STITCH

DMC		Anchor	
321	#	9046	Christmas red
535	◈	401	Very light ash gray
743	☆	302	Medium yellow
3747	∧	120	Very light blue violet
3814	%	1074	Aquamarine
blanc	·	2	White

FRENCH KNOT

DMC		Anchor	
blanc	●	2	White (3 strands)

BACKSTITCH

DMC		Anchor	
433	—	358	Medium brown
743	—	302	Medium yellow

Model was stitched on 14-count natural Aida fabric and is shown on a 5 x 6½-inch red photo album.

Welcome Kitty

Design Size: 64 wide x 89 high

CROSS-STITCH

DMC		Anchor	
162	V	9159	Ultra very dark blue
310	■	403	Black
317	♠	400	Pewter gray
350	✛	11	Medium coral
435	▲	1046	Very light brown
437	−	362	Light tan
739	↑	387	Ultra very light tan
754	(	1012	Light peach
761	I	1021	Light salmon
762	▣	234	Very light pearl gray
772	◂	259	Very light yellow green
922	✾	1003	Light copper
996	◪	433	Medium electric blue
blanc	~	2	White

FRENCH KNOT

DMC		Anchor	
310	●	403	Black (2 strands)
350	●	11	Medium coral (2 strands)

BACKSTITCH

DMC		Anchor	
310	—	403	Black
317	—	400	Pewter gray
347	—	1025	Very dark salmon
350	—	11	Medium coral (2 strands)
839	—	1086	Dark beige brown
975	—	355	Dark golden brown
			(2 strands for lettering)

Model was stitched on 14-count natural Aida fabric and is shown in an 8 x 10-inch frame with a green mat board.

For letters and numerals use chart below with dark golden brown (2 strands).

CROSS-STITCH

DMC		Anchor	
437		362	Light tan
498		1005	Dark Christmas red
738	2	361	Very light tan
742	☆	303	Light tangerine
772	—	259	Very light yellow green
813		161	Light blue
825	∪	162	Dark blue
890		218	Ultra dark pistachio green
987		244	Dark forest green
989	%	242	Forest green
3823	·	386	Ultra pale yellow

FRENCH KNOT

DMC		Anchor	
825	●	162	Dark blue

BACKSTITCH

DMC		Anchor	
825	—	162	Dark blue (2 strands)
938	—	381	Ultra dark coffee brown
987	—	244	Dark forest green (2 strands)

Model was stitched on 14-count antique white Aida fabric and is shown in a 10½ x 11-inch light yellow frame.

For lettering, use alphabets 2 through 5 on with dark blue (2 strands).

For numerals, use large numerals on page 69 with dark blue for cross-stitches and ultra dark coffee brown for backstitches.

Graduation Memories

Design Size: 81 wide x 67 high

CROSS-STITCH

DMC		Anchor	
437	⌘	362	Light tan
738	2	361	Very light tan
742	☆	303	Light tangerine
813	▣	161	Light blue
825	●	162	Dark blue
987	⬇	244	Dark forest green
3823	·	386	Ultra pale yellow

FRENCH KNOT

825	●	162	Dark blue

BACKSTITCH

498	—	1005	Dark Christmas red (2 strands)
742	—	303	Light tangerine (2 strands)
825	—	162	Dark blue (2 strands)
938	—	381	Ultra dark coffee brown

Model was stitched on 14-count antique white Aida fabric and is shown on a 5½ x 7½-inch journal with gold trim.

For lettering, use alphabet on page 72 with light blue cross-stitches and dark blue backstitches (2 strands).

Congratulations Graduate

Design Size: 105 wide x 114 high

CROSS-STITCH

DMC		Anchor	
310		403	Black
347		1025	Very dark salmon
433		358	Medium brown
435	//	1046	Very light brown
437		362	Light tan
498		1005	Dark Christmas red
535		401	Very light ash gray
738	2	361	Very light tan
743	L	302	Medium yellow
745	/	300	Light pale yellow
772	–	259	Very light yellow green
813		161	Light blue
825		162	Dark blue
840		1084	Medium beige brown
890		218	Ultra dark pistachio green
898		360	Very dark coffee brown
987		244	Dark forest green
989	%	242	Forest green
3712	4	1023	Medium salmon
3823	·	386	Ultra pale yellow

FRENCH KNOT

DMC		Anchor	
938	●	381	Ultra dark coffee brown

BACKSTITCH

498	—	1005	Dark Christmas red
938	—	381	Ultra dark coffee brown

Model was stitched on 14-count
antique white Aida fabric and is shown
in a 9½ x 11¼-inch mahogany frame.

For lettering and numerals, use alphabets
1 and 3 and small numerals on page 69 with
ultra dark coffee brown.

Just Married

Design Size: 70 wide x 70 high

CROSS-STITCH

DMC		Anchor	
208	◩	110	Very dark lavender
210	$	108	Medium lavender
211	╱	342	Light lavender
322	✖	978	Dark baby blue
3747	−	120	Very light blue violet

BACKSTITCH

208	—	110	Very dark lavender
792	—	941	Dark cornflower blue

LAZY DAISY

987	—	244	Dark forest green (for leaves, 2 strands)

Model was stitched on 14-count antique white Aida fabric and is shown in a 6½-inch square oak Sudberry box painted blue.

For lettering, use alphabet with dark cornflower blue.

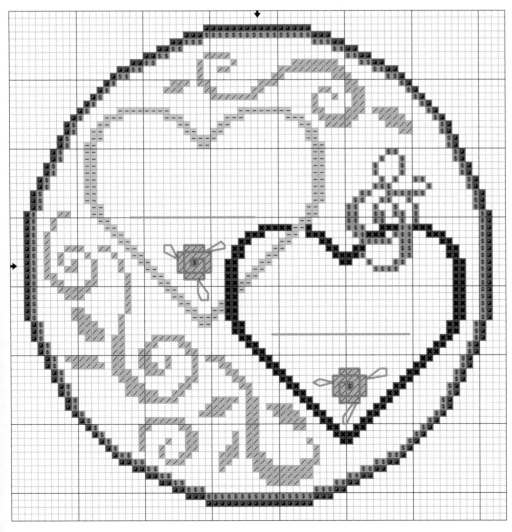

My Love

Design Size: 43 wide x 97 high

CROSS-STITCH

DMC		Anchor	
208	◩	110	Very dark lavender
210	$	108	Medium lavender
211	◿	342	Light lavender
322	✖	978	Dark baby blue
3747	–	120	Very light blue violet
3839	⦀	176	Medium lavender blue

BACKSTITCH

208	▬	110	Very dark lavender
3839	▬	176	Medium lavender blue

LAZY DAISY

987	▬	244	Dark forest green (for leaves, 2 strands)

Model was stitched on 14-count antique white Aida fabric and is shown in a 4¾ x 8¾-inch oak Sudberry box painted blue.

Bride & Groom Gift Tag

Design Size: 48 wide x 37 high

CROSS-STITCH

DMC		Anchor	
210	$	108	Medium lavender
645	♣	273	Very dark beaver gray
742	★	303	Light tangerine
744	1	301	Pale yellow
844	⬟	1041	Ultra dark beaver brown
948	O	1011	Very light peach
989	?	242	Forest green
3325	+	129	Light baby blue
3776	✿	1048	Light mahogany
blanc	·	2	White

FRENCH KNOT

335	●	38	Rose
792	●	941	Dark cornflower blue

BACKSTITCH

792	—	941	Dark cornflower blue
987	—	244	Dark forest green (2 strands)
blanc	—	2	White

Model was stitched on 14-count antique white Aida fabric and is shown on a 5 x 7-inch green gift card which has been covered with pastel decorative paper.

Wedding Cake Gift Tag

Design Size: 50 wide x 35 high

CROSS-STITCH

DMC		Anchor	
211	/	342	Light lavender
3326	↑	36	Light rose
3747	−	120	Very light blue violet
blanc	·	2	White

FRENCH KNOT

322	●	978	Dark baby blue

BACKSTITCH

208	—	110	Very dark lavender
335	—	38	Rose
792	—	941	Dark cornflower blue

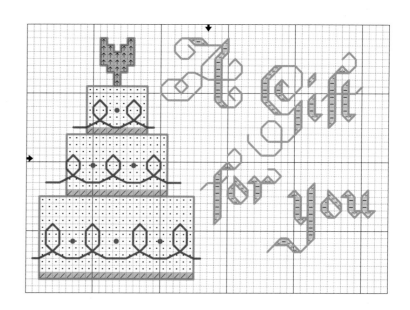

Model was stitched on 14-count antique white Aida fabric and is shown on a 5 x 7-inch pink gift card which has been covered with pastel decorative paper and trimmed with small purple flowers.

50th Anniversary

Design Size: 110 wide x 138 high

KREINIK BLENDED CROSS-STITCH

DMC/Kreinik		Anchor/Kreinik	
676/001	●●	891/001	Light old gold/Kreinik blending filament silver
729/001	■	890/001	Medium old gold/Kreinik blending filament silver
745/002	❯	300/002	Light pale yellow/Kreinik blending filament gold

BACKSTITCH

780	—	309	Ultra very dark topaz
782	—	307	Dark topaz

SMYRNA

677	▦	886	Very light old gold (2 strands)
782	▦	307	Dark topaz (2 strands)

Model was stitched on 14-count antique white Aida fabric and is shown in a 9 x 12-inch gold frame.

For lettering and numerals, use chart below with two strands of medium old gold mixed with one strand of Kreinik silver blending filament for cross-stitches, and dark topaz for backstitches.

Shaded area shows last two rows on previous page

Continue stitching from chart on next page

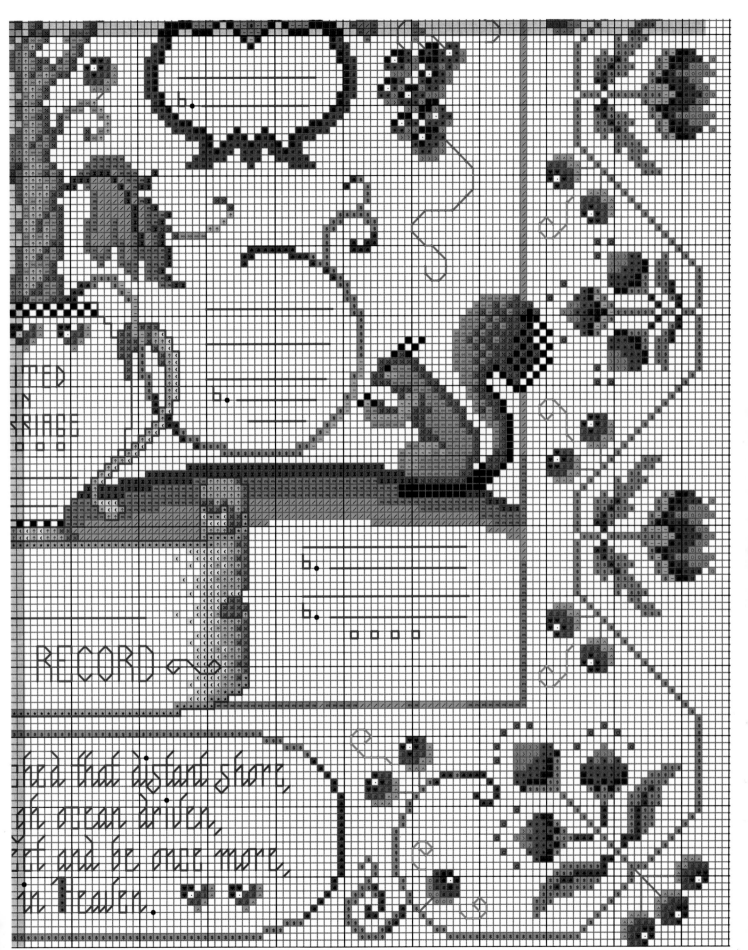

Shaded area shows last two rows on previous page

Reunion Circle

Design Size: 110 wide x 112 high

CROSS-STITCH

DMC		Anchor	
309	❂	42	Dark rose
310	■	403	Black
334	✿	977	Medium baby blue
335	↑	38	Rose
349	♥	13	Dark coral
414	8	235	Dark steel gray
415	<	398	Pearl gray
434	↓	310	Light brown
436	5	1045	Tan
553	✳	98	Violet
721	✿	925	Medium orange spice
738	7	361	Very light tan

CROSS-STITCH

DMC		Anchor	
743	☆	302	Medium yellow
745	6	300	Light pale yellow
754	∧	1012	Light peach
776	−	24	Medium pink
911	♣	205	Medium emerald green
954	+	203	Nile green
3325	1	129	Light baby blue
3823	/	386	Ultra pale yellow
blanc	·	2	White

FRENCH KNOT

DMC		Anchor	
312	●	979	Very dark baby blue
938	●	381	Ultra dark coffee brown

BACKSTITCH

DMC		Anchor	
553	−	98	Violet (2 strands)
743	−	302	Medium yellow (2 strands)
938	−	381	Ultra dark coffee brown (2 strands)
938	−	381	Ultra dark coffee brown

Model was stitched on 14-count antique white Aida fabric and is shown in a 12-inch square green frame with a 9-inch gold mat.

For lettering and numerals, use alphabet and large numerals on page 114 with tan cross-stitches and ultra dark coffee brown backstitches.

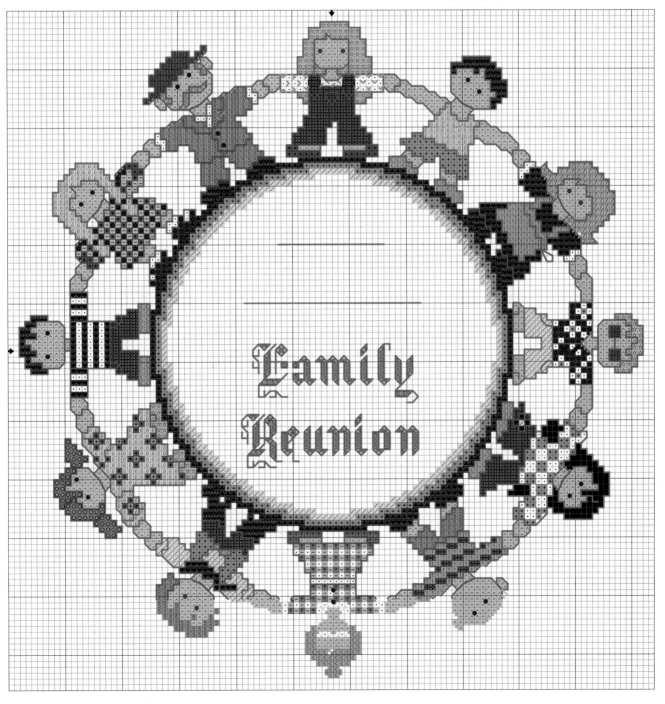

Reunion Map

Design Size: 138 wide x 110 high

CROSS-STITCH

DMC		Anchor	
210	)	108	Medium lavender
334	✤	997	Medium baby blue
436	5	1045	Tan
553	✱	98	Violet
677	2	886	Very light old gold
738	7	361	Very light tan
911	♣	205	Medium emerald green
954	+	203	Nile green
3325	1	129	Light baby blue

FRENCH KNOT

938	●	381	Ultra dark coffee brown

BACKSTITCH

743	➖	302	Medium yellow
899	➖	52	Medium rose
938	➖	381	Ultra dark coffee brown
938	➖	381	Ultra dark coffee brown (2 strands)

Model was stitched on 14-count antique white Aida fabric and is shown in a 9 x 12-inch silver frame. Flagged pins are used to mark where family members live.

For lettering, use alphabet on page 114 with tan cross-stitches and ultra dark coffee brown backstitches.

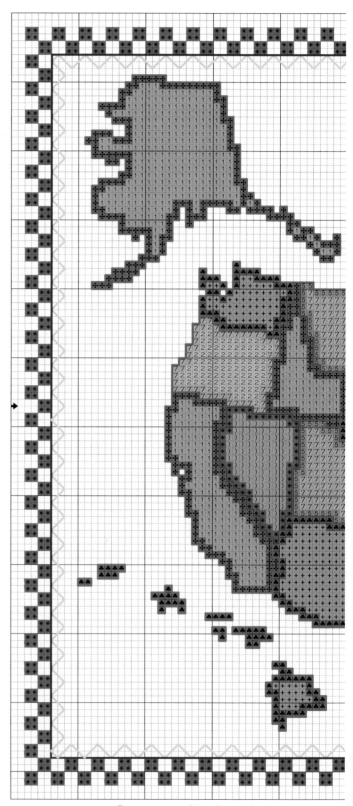

Continue stitching from chart on next page

First to Arrive

Design Size: 41 wide x 53 high

CROSS-STITCH

DMC		Anchor	
334	✚	977	Medium baby blue
743	☆	302	Medium yellow
745	6	300	Light pale yellow

FRENCH KNOT
938	●	381	Ultra dark coffee brown

BACKSTITCH
911	▬	205	Medium emerald green
938	▬	381	Ultra dark coffee brown
3607	▬	87	Light plum

Model was stitched on 14-count antique white Aida fabric and is shown in a 4 x 6-inch mahogany frame.

For numerals, use numerals on page 114 with rose 335/38 cross-stitches and ultra dark coffee brown backstitches.

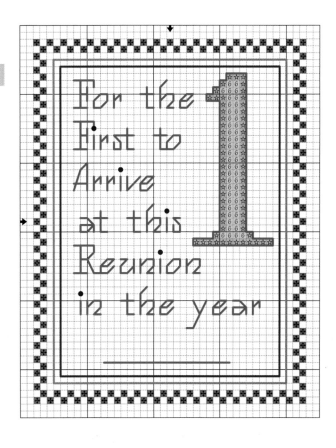

For the Oldest

Design Size: 35 wide x 53 high

CROSS-STITCH

DMC		Anchor	
312	■	979	Very dark baby blue
334	✚	977	Medium baby blue
3325	1	129	Light baby blue

BACKSTITCH
312	▬	979	Very dark baby blue
938	▬	381	Ultra dark coffee brown

Model was stitched on 14-count antique white Aida fabric and is shown in a 4 x 6-inch navy blue frame.

World's Greatest Mom

Design Size: 45 wide x 46 high

CROSS-STITCH

DMC		Anchor	
209		109	Dark lavender
310		403	Black
321		9046	Christmas red
402		1047	Very light mahogany
550		102	Very dark violet
552		99	Medium violet
718		88	Plum
798		131	Dark delft blue
809		130	Delft blue
815		43	Medium garnet
899		52	Medium rose
920		1004	Medium copper
986		246	Very dark forest green
989		242	Forest green
3823		386	Ultra pale yellow

BACKSTITCH

DMC		Anchor	
310		403	Black
920		1004	Medium copper
986		246	Very dark forest green

Model was stitched on 14-count natural Aida fabric and is shown in a 5-inch square black frame.

World's Greatest Brother

Design Size: 45 wide x 47 high

CROSS-STITCH

DMC		Anchor	
209		109	Dark lavender
310		403	Black
321		9046	Christmas red
402		1047	Very light mahogany
550		102	Very dark violet
552		99	Medium violet
718		88	Plum
798		131	Dark delft blue
809		130	Delft blue
815		43	Medium garnet
899		52	Medium rose
920		1004	Medium copper
986		246	Very dark forest green
989		242	Forest green
3823		386	Ultra pale yellow

BACKSTITCH

DMC		Anchor	
310		403	Black
920		1004	Medium copper

Model was stitched on 14-count natural Aida fabric and is shown in a 5-inch square black frame.

Through the Ages

Design Size: 135 wide x 144 high

CROSS-STITCH

DMC		Anchor	
209	>	109	Dark lavender
321	δ	9046	Christmas red
472	−	253	Ultra light avocado green
550	■	102	Very dark violet
552	✳	99	Medium violet
718	✿	88	Plum
796	■	133	Dark royal blue
798	▦	131	Dark delft blue
809	○	130	Delft blue
815	♥	43	Medium garnet
899	∧	52	Medium rose
915	▼	1029	Plum
986	▥	246	Very dark forest green
989	$	242	Forest green

CROSS-STITCH

DMC		Anchor	
3608	=	86	Very light plum
blanc	·	2	White

BACKSTITCH

DMC		Anchor	
796	—	133	Dark royal blue
809	—	130	Delft blue
920	—	1004	Medium copper
986	—	246	Very dark forest green

Model was stitched on 14-count natural Aida fabric and is shown in a 9 x 12-inch black frame.

For lettering, use alphabet and color key on this page.

ALPHABET KEY
CROSS-STITCH

DMC		Anchor	
796	■	133	Dark royal blue

BACKSTITCH

DMC		Anchor	
796	—	133	Dark royal blue
809	=	130	Delft blue

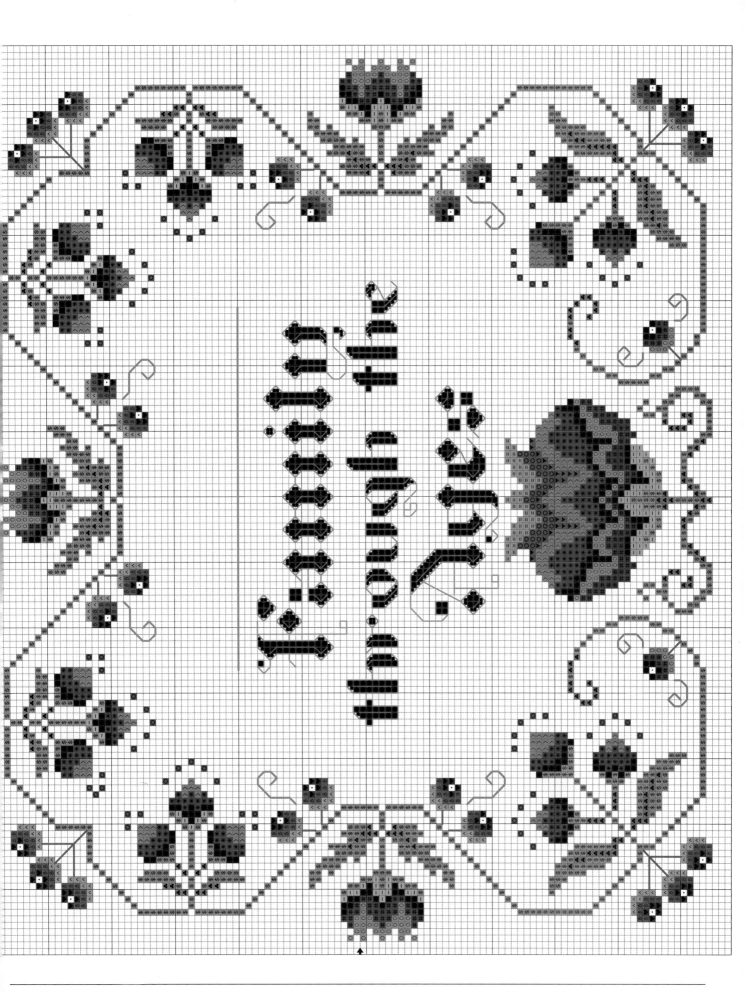

World's Greatest Daughter

Design Size: 48 wide x 46 high

CROSS-STITCH

DMC		Anchor	
209	⟩	109	Dark lavender
310	■	403	Black
321	δ	9046	Christmas red
402	~	1047	Very light mahogany
550	◆	102	Very dark violet
552	✳	99	Medium violet
718	✿	88	Plum
796	■	133	Dark royal blue
798	▦	131	Dark delft blue
809	⊙	130	Delft blue
815	◨	43	Medium garnet
899	∧	52	Medium rose
920	⁒	1004	Medium copper
986	■	246	Very dark forest green
989	$	242	Forest green
991	▨	1076	Dark aquamarine
3608	≡	86	Very light plum
3823	⟨	386	Ultra pale yellow

BACKSTITCH

DMC		Anchor	
310	▬	403	Black
920	▬	1004	Medium copper
986	▬	246	Very dark forest green

Model was stitched on 14-count natural Aida fabric and is shown in a 5-inch-square black frame.

World's Greatest Grandma

Design Size: 46 wide x 46 high

CROSS-STITCH

DMC		Anchor	
209	⟩	109	Dark lavender
310	■	403	Black
321	δ	9046	Christmas red
402	~	1047	Very light mahogany
550	◆	102	Very dark violet
552	✳	99	Medium violet
718	✿	88	Plum
796	■	133	Dark royal blue
798	▦	131	Dark delft blue
809	⊙	130	Delft blue
815	◨	43	Medium garnet
899	∧	52	Medium rose
920	⁒	1004	Medium copper
986	■	246	Very dark forest green
989	$	242	Forest green
3608	≡	86	Very light plum
3816	m	876	Medium celadon green
3823	⟨	386	Ultra pale yellow

BACKSTITCH

DMC		Anchor	
310	▬	403	Black
920	▬	1004	Medium copper

Model was stitched on 14-count natural Aida fabric and is shown in a 5-inch square black frame.

General Directions

WORKING FROM CHARTED DESIGNS

A square on a chart corresponds to a space for a Cross-Stitch on the stitching surface. The symbol in a square shows the floss color to be used for the stitch. The design stitch width and height are given; centers are shown by arrows. Backstitches are shown by straight lines and French Knots by dots.

FABRICS

Most of our photographed models were worked on 14-count Aida cloth from Charles Craft. Aida cloth is an evenweave fabric that has the same number of horizontal and vertical threads (or blocks of threads) per inch. That number is called the thread count.

The size of the design is determined by the size of the evenweave fabric on which you work. Use the chart below as a guide to determine the finished size of a design on various popular sizes of Aida cloth.

Thread Count	Number of Stitches in Design				
	10	20	30	40	50
11-count	1"	1¾"	2¾"	3⅝"	4½"
14-count	¾"	1⅜"	2⅛"	2⅞"	3⅝"
16-count	⅝"	1¼"	1⅞"	2½"	3⅛"
18-count	½"	1⅛"	1⅝"	2¼"	2¾"

(Measurements are given to the nearest ⅛".)

NEEDLES

A blunt-tipped tapestry needle, size 24 or 26, is used for stitching on 14-count fabrics. The higher the needle number, the smaller the needle. The correct-size needle is easy to thread with the amount of floss required, but is not so large that it will distort the holes in the fabric. The chart below indicates the appropriate-size needle for each size of fabric, along with the suggested number of strands of floss to use.

Fabric	Stitches Per Inch	Strands of Floss	Tapestry Needle Size
Aida	11	3	22 or 24
Aida	14	2	24 or 26
Aida	16	2	24, 26 or 28
Aida	18	1 or 2	26 or 28

THREADS

Our cover designs were stitched with DMC six-strand embroidery floss. Anchor floss numbers are also listed. The companies have different color ranges, so these are only suggested substitutions. Cut floss into comfortable working lengths—we suggest about 18 inches. Use two strands of floss to Cross-Stitch on a 14-count fabric unless otherwise noted in the color key. Use one strand of floss for Backstitches and French Knots.

GETTING STARTED

To begin in an unstitched area, bring threaded needle from back to front of fabric. Hold an inch of the end against the back, then hold it in place with your first few stitches. To end threads and begin new ones next to existing stitches, weave through the backs of several stitches.

THE STITCHES

Use two strands of floss for all Cross-Stitches, and one strand for Backstitches and French Knots, unless otherwise noted.

Cross-Stitch

The Cross-Stitch is formed in two motions. Follow the numbering in **Fig 1** and bring needle up at 1, down at 2, up at 3, down at 4, to complete the stitch. Work horizontal rows of stitches **(Fig 2)** wherever possible. Bring thread up at 1, work half of each stitch across the row, then complete the stitches on your return.

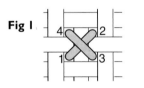

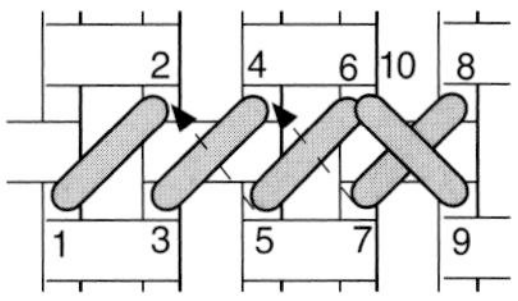

Quarter Cross-Stitch

Partial Cross-Stitches are used to create fine detail. They are named by the portion of the square stitching area that they occupy. The Quarter Cross-Stitch is made from any corner to the center of the square stitching area **(Fig 3)**. On the chart each quarter stitch is shown in the appropriate corner of the square as a tiny symbol; it represents the same color shown by the same full-sized symbol. Quarter stitches of different colors can be worked opposite each other, usually separated by a backstitch.

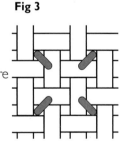

Backstitch

Backstitches are worked after Cross-Stitches have been completed. They may slope in any direction and are occasionally worked over more than one square of fabric. **Fig 4** shows the progression of several stitches; bring thread up at odd numbers and down at even numbers. Frequently you must choose where to end one Backstitch color and begin the next color.

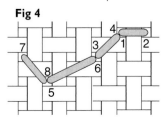

Choose the object that should appear closest to you. Backstitch around that shape with the appropriate color, then Backstitch the areas behind it with adjacent color(s).

French Knot

Bring thread up where indicated on chart. Wrap floss once around needle **(Fig 5)** and reinsert needle at 2, close to 1, but at least one fabric thread away from it. Hold wrapping thread tightly and pull needle through, letting thread go just as knot is formed. For a larger knot, use more strands of floss.

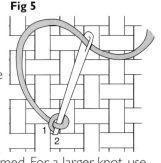

Fig 5

Straight Stitch

Straight Stitches can be made in any direction and over one or more squares of fabric. They can be used for details and decorations worked on top of an area of completed stitching. Bring needle up at one end of the stitch and down at the other end **(Fig 6).**

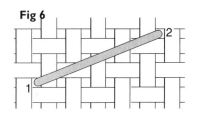

Fig 6

Running Stitch

The Running Stitch resembles basting. Bring thread up at odd numbers and down at even numbers **(Fig 7).** Follow direction shown on chart.

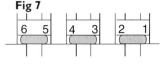

Fig 7

Lazy Daisy

This is a decorative stitch that is often worked on top of completed work. The chart will show the exact placement and length of each stitch **(Fig 8).** Bring needle up at 1, make a loop, and go down into same hole. Bring needle up at 2 inside the loop and pull gently to adjust the size and shape of the loop. Go down at 2 on the other side of the loop to secure. Be sure to anchor end especially well on the wrong side.

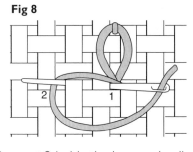

Fig 8

Smyrna Stitch

The Smyrna Stitch is a decorative stitch used to form

a star. Follow the numbering to work the diagonal stitches first, and then stitch a cross on top **(Fig 9).**

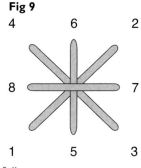

Fig 9

FINISHING

Wash stitched fabric in cool water with a gentle soap. Rinse well. Roll in a towel and squeeze out excess moisture. Place face down on a dry towel or padded surface and iron carefully.

PILLOW INSTRUCTIONS FOR BOY'S FIRST BIRTHDAY (PAGE 19)

To make pillow, use ½ yard of fabric for borders and backing and a 12-inch pillow insert. **Note:** *If using striped fabric as in the photographed model, you may need extra fabric to be sure pattern matches up properly.* Cut two 3 x 7-inch strips for sides, two 4 x 13-inch strips for top and bottom and one 13-inch square for backing. Trim stitched fabric to 9 x 7 inches. With right sides together, and using ½-inch seam allowances, sew side strips to stitched piece, then sew to top and bottom strips. Place top and backing pieces right sides together and stitch, leaving a 6-inch opening for turning. Turn right side out, insert pillow and whipstitch opening closed.

PILLOW INSTRUCTIONS FOR GIRL'S FIRST BIRTHDAY (PAGE 20)

To make pillow, use ½ yard of fabric for borders and backing and a 12-inch pillow insert. Cut two 3¾ x 9-inch strips for sides, two 3 x 13-inch strips for top and bottom and one 13-inch square for backing. Trim stitched fabric to 7½ x 9 inches. With right sides together, and using ½-inch seam allowances, sew side strips to stitched piece, then sew to top and bottom strips. Place top and backing pieces right sides together and stitch, leaving a 6-inch opening for turning. Turn right side out, insert pillow and whipstitch opening closed.

PILLOW INSTRUCTIONS FOR CELEBRATE (PAGE 24)

To make pillow, use ½ yard of fabric for borders and backing and a 12-inch pillow insert. Cut two 2½ x 8-inch strips for sides, two 3½ x 13-inch strips for top and bottom and one 13-inch square for backing. Trim stitched fabric to 10 x 8 inches. With right sides together, and using ½-inch seam allowances, sew side strips to stitched piece, then sew to top and bottom strips. Place top and backing pieces right sides together and stitch, leaving a 6-inch opening for turning. Turn right side out, insert pillow and whipstitch opening closed.